This is the
House
Where JacK
Lives

An I CAN READ Book ®

This is the House Where Jack Lives

by Joan Heilbroner

illustrated by Aliki

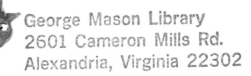

HarperCollins*Publishers*

To Sylvia and Eve

I Can Read Book is a registered trademark of
HarperCollins Publishers.

THIS IS THE HOUSE WHERE JACK LIVES
Text copyright © 1962 by Joan Heilbroner
Text copyright renewed 1990 by Joan Heilbroner
Illustrations copyright © 1962 by Aliki Brandenberg
Illustrations copyright renewed 1990 by Aliki Brandenberg

Library of Congress catalog card number: 62-7311
ISBN 0-06-022286-7 (lib. bdg.)

This is the
House
Where JacK
Lives

This is the house

Where Jack lives.

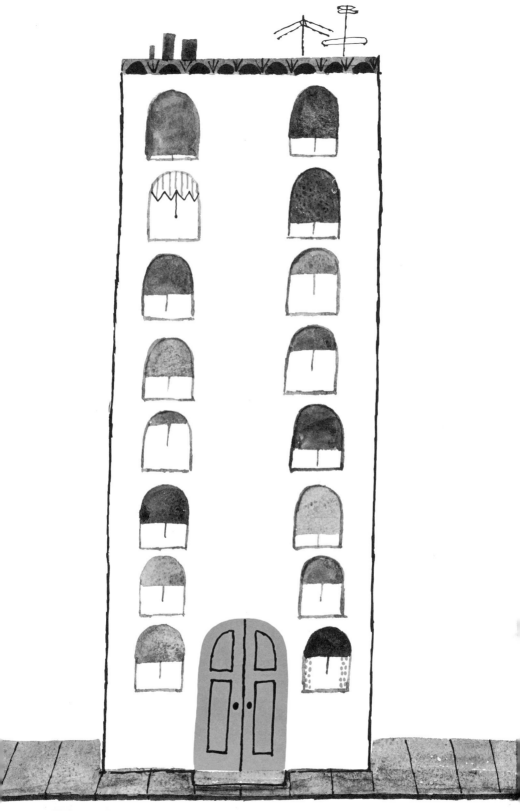

This is the dog

That lives in the house

Where Jack lives.

This is the boy

That walked the dog

That lives in the house

Where Jack lives.

This is the pail

That fell on the boy

That walked the dog

That lives in the house

Where Jack lives.

This is the man

That held the pail

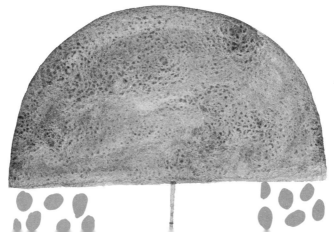

That fell on the boy

That walked the dog

That lives in the house

Where Jack lives.

This is the mop

So old and gray

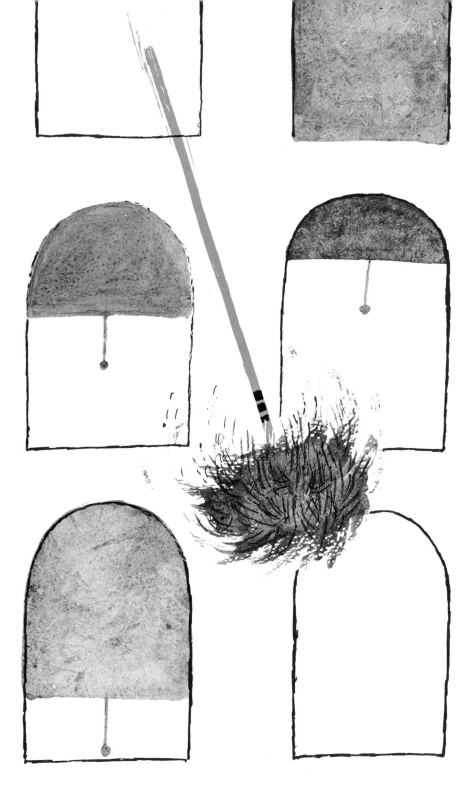

That bumped the man

That held the pail

That fell on the boy

That walked the dog

That lives in the house

Where Jack lives.

This is the girl

So fat and gay

That shook the mop

So old and gray

That bumped the man

That held the pail

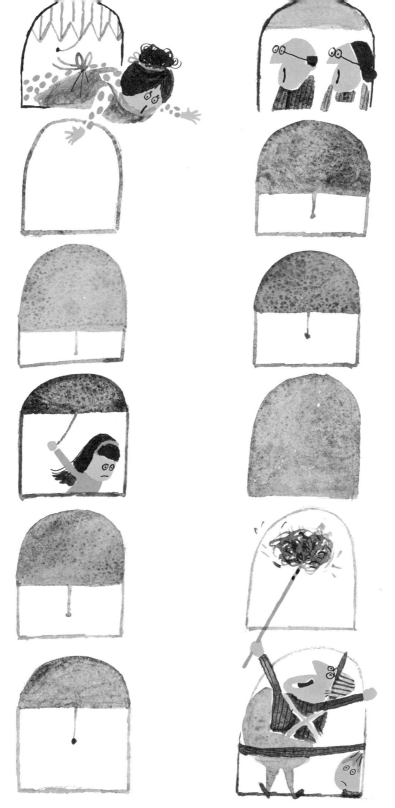

That fell on the boy

That walked the dog

That lives in the house

Where Jack lives.

This is the cat

That liked to play

That jumped on the girl

So fat and gay

That shook the mop

So old and gray

That bumped the man

That held the pail

That fell on the boy

That walked the dog

That lives in the house

Where Jack lives.

This is the cook

That had the tray

That fell on the cat

That liked to play

That jumped on the girl

So fat and gay

That shook the mop

So old and gray

That bumped the man

That held the pail

That fell on the boy

That walked the dog

That lives in the house

Where Jack lives.

This is the lady

in 7A

That rang for the cook

That had the tray

That fell on the cat

That liked to play

That jumped on the girl

So fat and gay

That shook the mop

So old and gray

That bumped the man

That held the pail

That fell on the boy

That walked the dog

That lives in the house

Where Jack lives.

This is the water

That one fine day

Came down on the lady

In 7A

That rang for the cook

That had the tray

That fell on the cat

That liked to play

That jumped on the girl

So fat and gay

That shook the mop

So old and gray

That bumped the man

That held the pail

That fell on the boy

That walked the dog

That lives in the house

Where Jack lives.

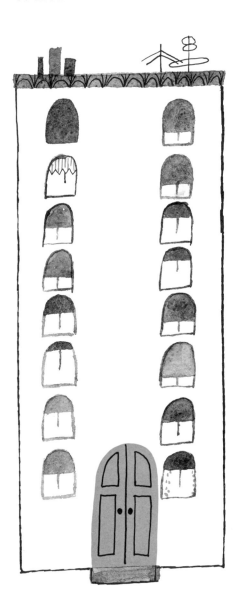

And this is Jack.

DATE DUE			

1406239

E
H

Heilbroner, Joan.

**This is the house
where Jack lives.**